THE MAGIC OF KINDNESS

by Autumn Rays

The Magic of Kindness
Published in 2022
Written by Autumn Rays

AR Book Publishing Ltd.
Registration Number 13797435

This purchase also represents another very important act of kindness: From every sale of this book, AR Book Publishing Ltd. will give 10% of the profit to charities that work globally to transform the lives of disadvantaged children and animals.

ISBN: 979-8-4246382-8-2

This book is dedicated to all the children spreading kindness to others with their good thoughts and deeds.

COOKIES

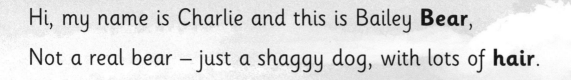

Hi, my name is Charlie and this is Bailey **Bear**,

Not a real bear – just a shaggy dog, with lots of **hair**.

I love to eat sweets and give Bailey Bear a **snuggle**,

but sometimes, when I'm tired, I do get into **trouble**.

Yesterday at school, when my friend went off to **play**,
I was hungry and I ate the sweets he forgot to put **away**.

When he came back, he was really very **mad**,

He told everyone in school, and that made me **sad**.

At home, I threw myself on the bed and started to **cry**.

Bailey Bear nuzzled my neck, and his sad eyes asked me **why**.

"My friends were angry because I did something bad", I **whined**.
Bailey Bear said, "The best thing to do is to always **be kind**."

Bailey Bear said:

"*Never steal food from another's bowl or growl at your **mum**.*

*Share your toys with others and you'll never be **glum**.*"

"If you do growl at your family or **friends**,

Then do something nice to make **amends**."

11

Later, when my mum tucked me **in**,
I gave her a hug and said with a **grin**,
*"Thanks to Bailey Bear, I learnt to try and be **kind**,
And never take something that is not **mine**."*

That night, I tossed and turned thinking all about **kindness**,

And the sun woke me up from my temporary **blindness**.

14

At school that day, I said sorry to my friend, and he was happy to **hear**,

That I had shared my biscuits with all our friends and Bailey **Bear**.

Later, in the playground I was tired and in a bad **mood**,
When Ella asked, "What's wrong?" I was terribly **rude**.

"You wouldn't understand," I said in an unkind **way**.
She said "I'm sorry you feel like that" and she turned **away**.

16

When I got home, my dad asked "Why are you **upset**?"
I said "I was tired and got mad at Ella, which I now **regret**."

"Apologise tomorrow," he said, "and I think you will **find**,
The best thing to do is to always be **kind**."

18

At school, I said sorry to Ella and explained my behaviour **yesterday**.

She said, "Apology accepted, would you like to come to my **birthday**?"

The next day my parents took me and Bailey Bear to the **party**.
Ella's house had balloons, a magician, cakes and **Smarties**.

Then the magician pulled a present from his hat for **me**.
I said *"But it is not my birthday, don't you **see**?"*

Ella said, *"I remember yesterday, when you were so down
and so **blue**,
So I asked the magician to magic up a gift just for **you**."*

And so, this is how my story ends. I learnt that the magic of kindness is that it lives in me and **you**.

If you show kindness to someone, it will always come back, trusted and **true**.

I learnt not to steal or be rude to my **friends**,

And I learnt that if I make a mistake, then I can always make **amends**.

Charlie says (with some help from Bailey Bear) that kindness is:

- Sharing with a friend (...preferably a juicy bone)

- Saying something kind (...like "*walkies*")

- Including others in your games (....and never biting their tails)

- Doing something nice for a special friend (...like scratching behind their ears)

Here are some ideas you can try to be kind. Why don't you pick one item from the list, so you can begin to practise kindness each day?

- Give someone a treat
- Send a thank-you note to someone
- Pick up rubbish on a walk
- Make a handmade gift for someone
- Give yourself a compliment
- Donate old books, toys or clothes
- Ask someone if they need help
- Have lunch with someone new in school
- Tell someone you know why they are awesome!

Thank you so much for purchasing this book. I hope you enjoyed meeting
Charlie and Bailey Bear and learning all about the magic of kindness
and how it can work for you.

If you enjoyed the book please leave a review on Amazon - It would be wonderful
to hear from you.

Keep an eye out as I will be back soon with more tales of adventure
from Charlie and Bailey Bear.

If you would like to be the first to hear about my next book,
please email me at autumn@autumnrays.com
and I will add your name to the advance notice list.

Printed in Poland
by Amazon Fulfillment
Poland Sp. z o.o., Wrocław